Because of Us

Why Outcomes Change When We Do

Mardoche Sidor, MD | Karen Dubin, PhD, LCSW |
SWEET Institute

SWEET Institute Publishing
Transformational Books for a Transformational World

Copyright © 2025 by the SWEET Institute

All rights reserved.

No part of this book may be reproduced, stored in a retrieval system, or transmitted in any form or by any means—electronic, mechanical, photocopying, recording, or otherwise—without the prior written permission of the publisher, except in the case of brief quotations embodied in critical articles or reviews.

Published by:
SWEET Institute Publishing
New York, NY
WWW.SWEETInstitute.com

First Edition
Printed in the United States of America

ISBN: (Paperback): 978-1-968105-08-2

Library of Congress Control Number: 2025942591

Cover Design by SWEET Institute Publishing
Interior Design and Layout by SWEET Institute Publishing

For bulk orders, permissions, or media inquiries, please contact:
contact@sweetinstitute.com

Unless otherwise noted, all stories and case examples in this book are either fictionalized or used with permission, and identifying details have been changed to protect the privacy of individuals.

SWEET Institute Publishing
Transformational Books for a Transformational World

Dedication

For every frontline worker who has stood in the fire and kept showing up.

For every clinician, case manager, peer, nurse, director, and advocate who has held hope—sometimes quietly, sometimes desperately—when no one else could.

For those who have sat with suffering, felt its weight, and still chose presence over retreat.

This book is for the ones who are brave enough to look within, who understand that healing is not just a service, it's a relationship; and that the most powerful intervention we offer is who we are.

And to those we serve—your courage rewrites the story of what's possible.

You remind us, again and again, why this work matters.

This book would not exist without you.

Other Books by Mardoche Sidor, M.D; Karen Dubin, PhD, LCSW; with the SWEET Institute

- Journey to Empowerment
- Discovering Your Worth: Everything You Need to Feel Fulfilled
- The Power of Faith: A Harvard-Trained Psychiatrist Speaking on Faith
- The Psychotherapy Certificate Course: The Clinician and Coach Manual (Books 1–3)
- The Anxiety Course: The Workbook
- What's Missing
- NLP for Clinicians
- 50 SWEET Poems: Reflections on life, love and self
- The Power of Belief: How Ideas Shape Leaders, Nations and the Future
- The Courage to Care: Stories of Healing, Hope, and the Power of Social Work: Told By Over 50 SWEET Institute Social Workers
- Transforming Team Relationships from the Inside Out: The SWEET Healing Circle for Agencies: Redefining Accountability, Collaboration, and Culture
- Remembering: The Journey Back to the Pre-Conditioned Self
- The Clinician's Mirror: A Story of Projection, Self-Awareness, and Transformation for Clinicians
- The Secret Is in Remembering: Why We Suffer, Why We Forget, and How to Return to Who We Are
- It's All Perfect: What If Nothing in Your Life Was a Mistake?

Table of Contents

Preface	7
Introduction	9
Why This Book	11
What This Book Is About	12
How to Read This Book	13
How This Book Works	14
Acknowledgments	15
Chapter 1 – The Invisible Variable	16
Chapter 2 – When We Don't Believe They Can Change	20
Chapter 3 – The Perception Loop: Belief as Prognosis	26
Chapter 4 – Bias Without Malice: The Blind Spots We Carry	31
Chapter 5 – What We Fail to See, Feel, and Do	36
Chapter 6 – The Myth of Neutrality	41
Chapter 7 – Unconditional Positive Regard—And Why It's So Rare	46
Chapter 8 – We Can't Give What We Don't Have	51
Chapter 9 – How Self-Regard Shapes Regard for Others	56
Chapter 10 – Soul-Searching in the Clinical Space	60
Chapter 11 – Inner Work as Professional Practice	64
Chapter 12 – From Fixing to Being With	68
Chapter 13 – Presence as Intervention	72
Chapter 14 – Belief as Medicine	76
Chapter 15 – Building a New Therapeutic Paradigm	80

Epilogue	84
Conclusion – We Are the Variable	85
A Note to the Reader	87
Final Acknowledgments	89
Reader Integration Toolkit	90
Appendix	92
Appendix A	93
Appendix B – SWEET Validation Framework	95
Recommended Reading	98
More from SWEET Institute Publishing	99
About the Authors	101

Preface

By Mardoche Sidor, MD

This book was born from a deep, ongoing question I could no longer ignore:

What if the greatest variable in healing has nothing to do with diagnosis, funding, or access—and everything to do with us?

I have spent decades working at the intersection of psychiatry, teaching, homelessness, private practice, trauma, academia, and community care. I have sat with individuals in their most vulnerable moments—when systems had failed them, when they had been misjudged, mislabeled, and forgotten.

And again and again, I saw something striking: People began to heal when they were believed in, when someone slowed down, and when someone stayed.

But I also saw something harder to name, that sometimes, people didn't get better—not because of what they lacked, but because of what we didn't bring—not enough presence, not enough belief, and not enough awareness of our own filters, wounds, and assumptions.

I have made mistakes. I have misread people. I have labeled instead of listened. I have rushed when I could have stayed still. This book is part of my own reflection, responsibility, and return to what really matters.

Because of Us is not just about clinical work — it's about human work. It is a call to all of us who serve to examine how we serve, and to understand that our presence is not neutral; rather, it heals, or it harms.

My hope is that this book becomes a mirror, a quiet companion in the hard moments, and a reminder that change is possible — not just in those we serve, but in us.

Because healing does not begin with a treatment plan. It begins with a person; and that person is you.

— Mardoche Sidor, MD

Introduction

By Karen Dubin, PhD, LCSW

I've been a social worker for over two decades, and in that time, one truth has become undeniable, healing is never just about what we do—it's about who we are.

Every person who walks into a room with someone in crisis carries with them a set of beliefs, a history, and an emotional atmosphere. These invisible forces—our biases, hopes, fears, and expectations—have just as much impact as any intervention or tool.

This book is a courageous and necessary call to look inward.

It asks us, gently but firmly, to recognize that we are part of the outcomes we see, that our tone, timing, and presence matter, and that people feel our belief in them—or our quiet doubt.

In clinical care, we often work with people who have been failed by systems, overlooked by institutions, and harmed by the very places meant to help them. To serve them well, we cannot stay on the surface. It is essential for us to bring our whole selves into the room and be willing to do the internal work that allows others to feel seen, safe, and held.

Because of Us is not a criticism—it is an offering. A gift to everyone brave enough to ask, *"What's my part in this?"* and a guide for how we can transform our care not by doing more, but by being more present, more aware, and more human.

It is rare to find a book that speaks to the heart, the science, and the soul of healing. This is one of those books.

I hope it finds you at just the right moment—and helps you find your way back to what matters most.

— **Karen Dubin, PhD, LCSW**

Why This Book

Because something essential is missing in how we talk about healing.

We focus on protocols, paperwork, symptoms, and outcomes — but rarely do we ask how we are part of the equation, not just professionally, but personally, internally, and humanly. This book exists to change that.

It's for the case manager rushing from one crisis to the next, wondering why some people seem stuck. It's for the clinician who follows every evidence-based practice but still feels something is missing. It's for the team leader who wants to inspire change but can't shake the burnout.

Because of Us was written to shine a light on the invisible variables that shape our work: our beliefs, our presence, our blind spots, and our capacity for self-awareness.

It challenges the myth that healing is only about the person in front of us — and instead shows how healing begins with how we show up to that person, again and again.

This book is not about blame. It's about responsibility. It's about reclaiming our power — not to control outcomes, but to contribute to transformation in real, measurable, and meaningful ways.

Because the outcomes we want to see depend, in part, on the courage we have to look within.

And when we do — when we understand our part — we become the medicine we've been waiting for.

What This Book Is About

This book is about the most powerful, and often overlooked, force in healing: us.

It's about the subtle but profound ways our beliefs, presence, and internal world shape the outcomes we see in others.

It explores the reality that we don't simply apply interventions—we are interventions. Our body language, tone of voice, assumptions, and attention (or lack thereof) communicate far more than we realize.

Because of Us is a practical and transformational guide for anyone in the helping professions. It is grounded in science, informed by clinical wisdom, and inspired by the lived experiences of those we serve.

This book does not offer easy answers—it offers honest reflections. It challenges the notion that we can stay emotionally distant or professionally detached and still expect meaningful connection or change.

Instead, it calls us back to what we intuitively know: healing happens in relationship; and relationships begin with presence, safety, belief, and regard. This book is about the truth that who we are matters just as much—if not more—than what we do.

And if we want to see different outcomes, we must be willing to see ourselves differently too.

How to Read This Book

This book is not meant to be rushed through. It is designed to be digested slowly, reflected on deeply, and returned to often. Each chapter is short for a reason—it is meant to offer a spark, a shift, a pause, something you can sit with during your commute, before a supervision session, or in a quiet moment between responsibilities.

You can read it cover to cover, or you can choose a chapter that speaks to what you're facing that day. There is no wrong order—only the invitation to read with openness, honesty, and curiosity.

This is not a textbook. It is a mirror. And the more you bring yourself to it, the more it will give back to you. Let it provoke you. Let it move you. Let it help you remember why you do this work—and who you are when you do it with intention.

Keep it nearby. Use it in team meetings. Bring it into supervision. Read it aloud with a colleague. Let it become part of the conversation.

Most of all, let it help you come home to the healing power you already carry inside you.

How This Book Works

This book is structured around short, potent chapters that each illuminate a core truth about the relationship between our inner world and the healing process.

You'll notice that many chapters begin with a provocation or reflection. They are meant to disrupt automatic thinking, challenge hidden assumptions, and open space for insight.

Chapters are followed by moments of pause — opportunities to reflect, question, and apply the message to your real-world work and relationships.

Scientific research and psychological theory are woven throughout, but never at the expense of clarity or accessibility. This book is for everyone — from peer specialists and case managers to therapists, nurses, and leaders.

You will also find tools, stories, and applications that can be used in supervision, team discussions, and training. Think of this book as a portable companion — a guide for the journey of inner awareness and outer transformation.

It is not a book you finish. It is a book you return to — again and again — as you grow, stumble, and recommit to the work that matters most.

Acknowledgments

This book would not exist without the extraordinary individuals who remind us—every single day—why this work matters.

To the frontline staff, case managers, clinicians, peer specialists, nurses, housing and shelter workers—you are the heartbeat of this book. Your presence, your persistence, and your willingness to show up when it's hardest are what inspired every word.

To the people we serve—you are our greatest teachers. Thank you for your courage, your honesty, and your humanity.

To the leadership and staff throughout the field—thank you for believing in the mission, and for the quiet, often invisible work of transformation that happens because of your consistency and care.

To my colleagues, mentors, and co-authors—thank you for your insight, your rigor, and your shared commitment to the deeper layers of healing.

And to everyone who dares to ask the hardest question of all, *"What is my part in all this?"* this book is yours.

Chapter 1 – The Invisible Variable

"The success of any healing encounter does not begin with the treatment plan – it begins with the mind, heart, and belief of the one offering it."

We are trained to look outward. We gather histories. We assess for symptoms. We document behaviors, diagnoses, and interventions. We create treatment plans, make referrals, and measure progress. But rarely do we ask: What am I bringing into this interaction? What beliefs am I holding about this person? What story am I unconsciously projecting onto them? Do I actually believe they can change?

This unspoken variable—us—shapes the entire trajectory of care. When a person isn't improving, we often assume it's because of them:

- They're not ready.
- They're resistant.
- They're unmotivated.
- They're too complex.

But what if, instead, we dared to ask: What might be happening because of us?

What if it's not that they're unmotivated, but that they're sensing—on some deep, unspoken level—that we don't believe in their transformation?

Research shows that our expectations directly affect outcomes—a phenomenon known as the Pygmalion effect

(Rosenthal & Jacobson, 1968). When clinicians hold high expectations for their patients, outcomes tend to improve.

In psychotherapy, the therapist's belief in the client's capacity for change is among the most powerful predictors of success (Wampold, 2015).

Framework: The Healing Equation

Outcome — Client Variables — Clinician Variables

Human beings are exquisitely attuned to belief. They feel it in our tone, in our body language, in our gaze. In the level of enthusiasm we carry when we walk into the room.

This is not about blame. It's about responsibility. There is a precious difference. We are not the cause of someone's suffering; but we are part of the relational field in which healing can either emerge or remain stunted.

Studies show that clinicians are not immune to implicit bias. Research by Fitzgerald & Hurst (2017) found strong evidence of implicit bias in healthcare providers, which can influence diagnosis and treatment.

Bias shows up in what we focus on, what we omit, how long we listen, and how deeply we attune.

Carl Rogers emphasized that unconditional positive regard is essential to healing (Rogers, 1957). Clinicians who have not explored their own beliefs and wounds may struggle to offer this regard.

Clinician self-awareness is directly linked to greater clinical effectiveness (Jennings & Skovholt, 1999).

We are the intervention. We are the method. We are the medicine. Healing begins when we take off our filters, not just to see the person more clearly, but to see ourselves.

FOUR FORCES OF INFLUENCE

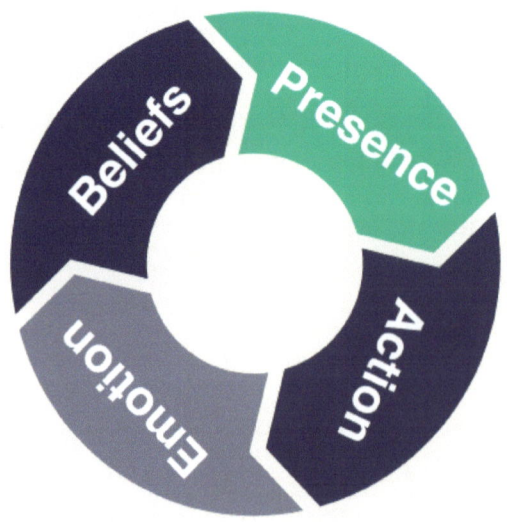

Reflection Prompts

- Think of someone you're working with who is 'not making progress.' What do you believe about them? Are there any assumptions you're carrying that might need to be questioned?
- Do you truly believe this person can change? What would change in your approach if you did?

References

- FitzGerald, C., & Hurst, S. (2017). Implicit bias in healthcare professionals: A systematic review. BMC Medical Ethics, 18(1), 19.
- Horvath, A. O., Del Re, A. C., Flückiger, C., & Symonds, D. (2011). Alliance in individual psychotherapy. Psychotherapy, 48(1), 9–16.
- Jennings, L., & Skovholt, T. M. (1999). The cognitive, emotional, and relational characteristics of master therapists. Journal of Counseling Psychology, 46(1), 3–11.
- Rogers, C. R. (1957). The necessary and sufficient conditions of therapeutic personality change. Journal of Consulting Psychology, 21(2), 95–103.
- Rosenthal, R., & Jacobson, L. (1968). Pygmalion in the classroom: Teacher expectation and pupils' intellectual development. Holt, Rinehart & Winston.
- Wampold, B. E. (2015). How important are the common factors in psychotherapy? An update. World Psychiatry, 14(3), 270–277.

Chapter 2 – When We Don't Believe They Can Change

"To believe in someone is to create the conditions for their transformation. To doubt them is to reinforce the very patterns we're trying to help them change."

Every day, without speaking a word, we convey messages:

- *"I believe in you."*
- *"You are capable."*
- *"You are more than your diagnosis."*

Or the opposite:

- *"You're broken."*
- *"You won't change."*
- *"You're just like the others."*

The belief we hold—even unconsciously—sets the stage for what is possible.

Belief vs. Doubt in Practice

Dimension	Belief Present	Doubt Present
Tone	Warm, hopeful	Flat, skeptical
Engagement	Invested and collaborative	Withholding or avoidant
Action Taken	Consistent, empowering	Minimal, directive
Client Response	Opens, reflects, tries	Withdraws, resists, stagnates

A wealth of evidence confirms the power of the self-fulfilling prophecy in human development. When we expect failure, we often find it. When we expect growth, we often foster it. This is especially true in therapeutic, educational, and medical relationships.

In their groundbreaking study, Rosenthal and Jacobson (1968) found that teachers' expectations could influence students' intellectual growth, simply because of the way they interacted with them. Our clients don't become who we hope—they often become who we subtly expect. (Rosenthal & Rubin, 1978; Snyder, 1984)

The brain is not static. It is plastic—shaped by experience, environment, and relationship. Neuroplasticity research shows that belief, attention, and relational attunement can physically alter neural pathways (Doidge, 2007; Siegel, 2012).

The therapeutic relationship—when grounded in trust, empathy, and belief—activates brain regions associated with safety, learning, and growth (Schore, 2012).

"Safety is the treatment." (Porges, 2011). But safety is not just about environment. It's about being felt, seen, and held in a relationship that expects your growth—not your stagnation.

Clinicians may not intend harm. But a pattern emerges:

- When someone struggles to follow through, we label them "non-compliant."
- When someone questions us, we call them "resistant."
- When someone relapses, we say they're "not ready."

These are not neutral terms. They are laden with implication—and often, they hide our own frustration, helplessness, or even quiet disbelief. Research by Sue et al. (2009) found that clinicians' assumptions about client motivation or resistance were often inaccurate and more reflective of clinician bias than client behavior.

When we don't believe people can change, we lower the bar. We give shorter sessions, fewer opportunities. We rush the intake and skim the notes. We start planning discharge the moment someone misses an appointment. Without realizing it, we participate in the very systems that keep people stuck.

 To believe in someone is not to deny their struggle. It is to hold space for both their pain and their possibility. It is to look at someone who has been dismissed by every system and say: *"You are more than what has happened to you."*

This belief does not require false hope. It requires grounded hope—an attitude of deep regard combined with practical action.

According to Snyder et al. (1991), hope itself is composed of two ingredients: the belief that change is possible, and the strategies to move toward it.

In one study on motivational interviewing, Miller and Rollnick (2013) found that therapists who demonstrated a strong belief in their client's capacity for change had significantly better outcomes than those who remained neutral or pessimistic.

What we believe shows up. And what we believe gets built.

Reflection Prompts
- Think of a time when you quietly doubted someone's ability to change. How did it affect the way you engaged with them?
- How might your attitude or language shift if you genuinely believed in the person's potential for transformation?
- Do you believe in your own capacity for change? How does that affect your work with others?

References
- Doidge, N. (2007). The brain that changes itself: Stories of personal triumph from the frontiers of brain science. Viking.
- Miller, W. R., & Rollnick, S. (2013). Motivational Interviewing: Helping People Change (3rd ed.). Guilford Press.
- Porges, S. W. (2011). The polyvagal theory: Neurophysiological foundations of emotions, attachment, communication, and self-regulation. W. W. Norton & Company.
- Rosenthal, R., & Jacobson, L. (1968). Pygmalion in the classroom: Teacher expectation and pupils' intellectual development. Holt, Rinehart & Winston.
- Rosenthal, R., & Rubin, D. B. (1978). Interpersonal expectancy effects: The first 345 studies. Behavioral and Brain Sciences, 1(3), 377–386.
- Schore, A. N. (2012). The science of the art of psychotherapy. W. W. Norton & Company.

- Siegel, D. J. (2012). The developing mind: How relationships and the brain interact to shape who we are. Guilford Press.
- Snyder, C. R. (1984). The psychology of hope. Jossey-Bass.
- Snyder, C. R., Rand, K. L., & Sigmon, D. R. (1991). Hope theory: A member of the positive psychology family. In Lopez, S. J. & Snyder, C. R. (Eds.), The Oxford Handbook of Positive Psychology (pp. 257–276). Oxford University Press.
- Sue, S., Cheng, J. K. Y., Saad, C. S., & Chu, J. P. (2012). Asian American mental health: A call to action. American Psychologist, 67(7), 532–544.

Chapter 3 – The Perception Loop: Belief as Prognosis

"What we expect, we notice. What we notice, we reinforce. What we reinforce, becomes reality."

Belief Doesn't Just Follow Evidence—It Creates It

In most disciplines, we are taught to be objective—to observe, to measure, and to act based on what we see. But in human healing, what we see is inseparable from what we believe.

We do not simply observe the world; we interpret it through the lens of our past experiences, training, expectations, and emotional state. And that interpretation determines what we notice, what we overlook, how we feel, and what we do next.

This is the perception loop:

- We believe something.
- That belief affects what we see.
- What we see reinforces what we feel.
- What we feel influences what we do.
- What we do confirms the original belief.

REAL-WORLD EXAMPLES OF PERCEPTION LOOPS

INITIAL BELIEF	PERCEPTION	EMOTIONAL RESPONSE	ACTION TAKEN	RESULT/ REINFORCEMENT
THEY'RE RESISTANT	They're not following through	Frustration	Limit time, use directive tone	Client withdraws, confirms 'resistance'
THEY'RE MANIPULATIVE	They changed their story	Suspicion	Avoid emotional engagement	Client becomes defensive, confirms bias
THEY'RE NOT MOTIVATED	They missed group again	Disappointment	Stop offering options	Client disengages further
THEY'RE COMPLEX BUT CAPABLE	They showed up upset	Empathy	Explore underlying cause	Client opens up and builds trust
THEY'RE IN SURVIVAL MODE	They yelled at staff	Compassion	Stay calm, validate experience	De-escalation and future trust

This table illustrates common perception loops in practice — how our initial beliefs can shape our perceptions, emotional responses, actions, and ultimately, reinforce the original belief.

It is not just the person in treatment who is in a loop. We are in one, too.

Cognitive Bias and Clinical Practice

Cognitive science confirms that our minds are not neutral information processors — they are pattern-seeking, meaning-making machines. Once we form a belief, our brains filter data through that belief, prioritizing confirming information, and discarding what doesn't fit (Nickerson, 1998). This is known as confirmation bias.

In clinical care, this bias can be dangerous. If we believe a person is manipulative, we will begin to interpret even their genuine efforts through that lens. If we believe a person is not capable of insight, we may unconsciously minimize their moments of clarity.

One study found that diagnostic labels significantly influenced clinicians' perceptions of behavior. Identical case descriptions were interpreted more negatively when labeled "schizophrenic" than when labeled "depressed" (Langer & Abelson, 1974). That label, like all beliefs, changed the lens.

Belief as Prognosis

This loop isn't just theoretical. It affects real lives. When we believe someone is not likely to improve, we often:
- Lower our expectations.
- Offer fewer opportunities.
- Document more deficits than strengths.
- Shift from curiosity to control.
- Move from collaboration to compliance-based approaches.

This becomes a self-fulfilling prophecy. According to research in psychotherapy outcome studies, clinician expectations are one of the most consistent predictors of client progress—regardless of modality (Constantino et al., 2021).

The belief we hold becomes the prognosis we give. And that prognosis becomes the story they live.

The Lens We Carry

The perception loop doesn't only apply to people we serve. It applies to everyone—colleagues, family members, even ourselves.

If we believe someone is difficult, we see more difficulty. If we believe someone is rigid, we stop seeing their vulnerability. If we believe we ourselves are not enough, we begin to treat others from a place of deficiency rather than presence.

In many ways, healing work is not just about helping others rewrite their story—it's about recognizing the story we're telling ourselves about them.

Breaking the Loop

To break the perception loop, we are to disrupt the chain at its origin: belief.

This doesn't mean denying reality. It means choosing to see the full reality, including strength, resilience, and possibility—even when it's not obvious.

Neuroscience supports this shift. When we practice cognitive reappraisal—intentionally reframing how we perceive others—we engage the prefrontal cortex and downregulate the amygdala, increasing emotional regulation and empathy (Ochsner & Gross, 2005).

Belief is not a soft concept. It's a neurological, relational, and clinical intervention.

We Become What We Expect

Belief is not passive. It is participatory.

When we believe in someone's healing, we are not simply offering hope. We are anchoring a neural, emotional, and interpersonal process that says: *"You are already becoming."*

And when we believe in ourselves — our own worth, capacity, and clarity — we interrupt the loops that have kept us stuck, too.

Our perception is not truth. It is a story. And we can choose to tell a better one.

Reflection Prompts

- Think of someone who frustrates you. What belief might be shaping how you see them?
- Where might you be trapped in a perception loop — with a client, a colleague, or yourself?
- What would shift if you saw them (or yourself) through a different lens?

References

- Constantino, M. J., Coyne, A. E., & Boswell, J. F. (2021). Therapist expectations and treatment outcomes: A self-fulfilling prophecy? Psychotherapy, 58(1), 1–12.
- Langer, E. J., & Abelson, R. P. (1974). A patient by any other name: Clinician group differences in labeling bias. Journal of Consulting and Clinical Psychology, 42(1), 4–9.
- Nickerson, R. S. (1998). Confirmation bias: A ubiquitous phenomenon in many guises. Review of General Psychology, 2(2), 175–220.
- Ochsner, K. N., & Gross, J. J. (2005). The cognitive control of emotion. Trends in Cognitive Sciences, 9(5), 242–249.

Chapter 4 – Bias Without Malice: The Blind Spots We Carry

"The most dangerous bias is the one we don't know we have."

Bias is not always loud. It doesn't always look like prejudice or sound like hate. In fact, some of the most powerful biases are quiet, subtle, and unconscious.

In clinical and helping professions, we pride ourselves on objectivity, fairness, and empathy. But every one of us carries filters—shaped by our culture, training, upbringing, and unresolved experiences.

These filters form the basis of our blind spots. And the danger of a blind spot is not just that we don't see it—it's that we don't know we're not seeing it.

Research has shown that even well-intentioned, compassionate providers can hold implicit biases that affect diagnosis, treatment planning, and interpersonal dynamics (FitzGerald & Hurst, 2017).

This isn't about being bad. It's about being human.

One of the most insidious aspects of unconscious bias is that it often hides behind clinical language. We call people 'resistant,' 'non-compliant,' or 'borderline,' not realizing we may be reacting to something within ourselves—frustration, helplessness, fear.

When we're unaware of our own internal responses, we unconsciously project them onto the people we serve.

In psychoanalysis, this is known as countertransference — our emotional reactions to another person based not just on their behavior, but on our unresolved internal material (Gabbard, 2001).

Unchecked countertransference doesn't just distort how we see others — it distorts how we treat them.

Our blind spots influence:
- Who we give more time to
- Who we avoid
- Who we assume will improve — and who we don't
- Who we speak gently to — and who we speak down to
- Who we over-identify with — and who we judge

Bias can show up as under-engagement just as easily as over-involvement.

For example, we may unknowingly withdraw from someone whose pain mirrors our own. Or we may become overly invested in someone whose story activates our need to rescue.

Both responses are forms of bias. And both are to be acknowledged if we are to provide truly person-centered care.

Implicit Association Tests (IATs) have revealed that even individuals who explicitly endorse egalitarian beliefs often exhibit automatic preferences at the subconscious level (Greenwald et al., 1998).

This includes biases around race, gender, age, body size, diagnosis, socioeconomic status, and trauma history.

Table: Types of Bias Common in Helping Professions

The following table outlines common cognitive and emotional biases that often show up unconsciously in mental health, healthcare, and human services professionals. These biases can impact how we assess, engage, interpret, and intervene—even when our intentions are good.

BIAS TYPE	DESCRIPTION	IMPACT ON PRACTICE
Confirmation Bias	Favoring information that confirms pre-existing beliefs or expectations.	We miss signs of change or improvement that don't fit the narrative.
Diagnostic Overshadowing	Attributing all symptoms to a known diagnosis, overlooking other factors.	People are seen only through their label.
Cultural Bias	Interpreting behaviors through the lens of one's own cultural norms.	Misreading communication, family dynamics, or expression of distress.
Socioeconomic Bias	Assuming motivations or values based on economic status.	Judging choices or behaviors as irresponsible without context.
Gender Bias	Applying stereotyped assumptions based on gender identity or expression.	Minimizing symptoms or misinterpreting assertiveness.
Racial Bias	Unconscious attitudes or stereotypes based on race or ethnicity.	Over-pathologizing, underestimating pain, or misjudging behavior.
Transference/ Countertransference Bias	Reacting to clients based on our own emotional history.	Projection onto clients leads to distorted interpretations.

Awareness is the first step—but not the last.

When we become aware of our blind spots, we have a choice: to defensively protect our image or to courageously deepen our integrity.

Blind spots are not a failure. They are an invitation.

They ask us to slow down, reflect, and become more honest with ourselves—for the sake of those we serve.

To reduce harm, we are to recognize where our perceptions end, and the other person's reality begins.

This is humility in action. And it is the foundation of ethical care.

Reflection Prompts

- Can you identify a time when your reaction to someone may have come from your own unresolved material?
- What diagnoses or behaviors activate judgment or discomfort in you? Where might those reactions be coming from?
- How can you build regular self-inquiry into your practice to catch blind spots before they cause harm?

Reflection Chart: From Blind Spot to Insight

Use this tool to identify and explore a potential blind spot. The goal is not to judge yourself, but to grow in awareness and integrity.

Reflection Prompt	Your Notes
What is one recent moment where I felt frustrated or disconnected from someone I serve?	
What belief or assumption might I have been holding about that person?	
Where might that belief come from in my own experience?	
What bias might have influenced my reaction?	
How might I reframe or expand my understanding moving forward?	
What is one action I can take to practice more presence and less projection?	

References

- FitzGerald, C., & Hurst, S. (2017). Implicit bias in healthcare professionals: A systematic review. BMC Medical Ethics, 18(1), 19.
- Gabbard, G. O. (2001). A contemporary psychoanalytic model of countertransference. Journal of Clinical Psychology, 57(8), 983–991.
- Greenwald, A. G., McGhee, D. E., & Schwartz, J. L. K. (1998). Measuring individual differences in implicit cognition: The implicit association test. Journal of Personality and Social Psychology, 74(6), 1464–1480.

Chapter 5 – What We Fail to See, Feel, and Do

"Healing often breaks down not because of what we do wrong — but because of what we fail to do at all."

In helping professions, we are taught to act, to do, to solve, to respond.

But some of the most consequential moments in care are not shaped by what we do, but by what we fail to see, fail to feel, and therefore fail to do.

What we do not see in someone's story—their strength, their subtle bids for connection, their masked grief, can mean the difference between progress and disconnection.

What we fail to feel—the sadness behind the anger, the fear behind the resistance, can mean the difference between attunement and misunderstanding.

What we fail to do—pause, ask, reflect, repair, can leave the person feeling unseen, unheard, and unchanged.

Clinical omissions are often harder to detect than errors. They're not usually documented. They don't show up in progress notes. But their impact is profound.

Researchers call this phenomenon the 'error of omission.' In medicine, it refers to a failure to act when necessary. In psychotherapy, it shows up as a failure to inquire, to validate, to connect (Schachter, 2008).

Omission bias — our tendency to judge harmful inaction as less blameworthy than harmful action — can allow these failures to go unexamined (Baron & Ritov, 2004).

Framework: The Omission Impact Model

This framework illustrates how what we fail to notice, name, or address can result in unintended harm or disconnection. It reminds us that silence and inaction carry weight — and are often interpreted through the lens of past trauma or systemic neglect.

A clinician may avoid difficult conversations with a person experiencing loss because of their own discomfort with grief. A therapist may not address racial identity in a cross-cultural session out of fear of 'saying the wrong thing.'

But in both cases, the silence is felt.

Unspoken moments are never neutral. In healing work, they are interpreted, often through the lens of the person's past wounds.

When something important is not acknowledged, the implicit message becomes: 'It doesn't matter.' Or worse: 'You don't matter.'

Attachment research shows that one of the key predictors of secure connection is the caregiver's ability to notice and respond to subtle cues (Ainsworth et al., 1978). The same applies in therapeutic relationships.

Our attunement—what we perceive, reflect, and respond to, signals safety and worth.

Conversely, repeated failures to notice someone's inner world mirror early patterns of misattunement, abandonment, or neglect.

This is how clinical omissions can become re-enactments of past trauma.

This is not about becoming perfect. It is about becoming present.

Presence means slowing down. Paying attention. Practicing deep listening, not just to the words, but to the pauses, the body, the atmosphere.

Presence also means noticing ourselves: when we're distracted, defensive, or emotionally checked out. These internal states often correlate with moments of omission.

By building self-awareness, we can begin to close the gap between what's needed and what's offered. Between what someone longs for and what they receive.

Healing requires action. But the most powerful actions are born from perception—and perception requires presence.

Table: Common Omissions and Their Unintended Consequences

The table below offers examples of common oversights in care, what is missed, and how it might impact the people we serve.

Omission	What Was Missed	Unintended Consequence
Didn't ask about recent loss	Grief and vulnerability	Person feels unseen or unsupported
Skipped follow-up after a crisis	Ongoing distress or need for reassurance	Loss of trust or increased risk
Ignored body language	Emotional overwhelm or shutdown	Missed opportunity for de-escalation
Didn't explore meaning behind resistance	Fear, shame, or past trauma	Interpretation of manipulation or non-compliance
Rushed the conversation	Client's unspoken priorities or strengths	Reinforcement of systemic dismissal
Avoided discussing identity or culture	Lived experience of marginalization	Sense of erasure or microaggression

Reflection Prompts

- Think of a recent encounter where you felt something important was missed. What might you have failed to see or feel?
- Are there topics or emotions you tend to avoid in your work? What might be underlying that avoidance?
- What would change if you prioritized presence over performance in your healing work?

References

- Ainsworth, M. D. S., Blehar, M. C., Waters, E., & Wall, S. (1978). Patterns of Attachment: A Psychological Study of the Strange Situation. Lawrence Erlbaum Associates.
- Baron, J., & Ritov, I. (2004). Omission bias, individual differences, and normality. Organizational Behavior and Human Decision Processes, 94(2), 74–85.
- Schachter, D. L. (2008). The Seven Sins of Memory: Insights From Psychology and Cognitive Neuroscience. American Psychologist, 54(3), 182–203.

Chapter 6 – The Myth of Neutrality

"There is no such thing as neutrality when it comes to human relationship. Silence speaks. Absence speaks. Everything we do, and don't do, communicates something."

In clinical training, we are often taught to be neutral. To be the blank slate. The reflective surface. The steady presence in the storm.

But neutrality is a myth.

We are always communicating something. Through our body language, our tone, our timing, our curiosity, or lack thereof.

What we ask and what we avoid. What we document and what we ignore. All of it reveals our positioning, our values, our beliefs.

To claim neutrality is often to overlook the real and subtle ways in which our identity, culture, race, gender, and history shape how we perceive and engage with others.

It can be a defense mechanism—a way of avoiding discomfort, difficult topics, or the emotional vulnerability of genuine engagement.

In the therapeutic space, attempts at neutrality often come across not as calm, but as cold; and not as professional, but as distant. That distance, in turn, can trigger deep wounds, especially for individuals whose lives have been marked by disconnection, dismissal, or neglect.

Research on therapeutic alliance consistently shows that the quality of the relationship is one of the strongest predictors of outcome (Horvath et al., 2011). And yet, neutrality does not build alliance; rather, attunement does, engagement does, and warmth does.

This is especially true when working with individuals from historically marginalized or oppressed backgrounds.

According to Sue et al. (2007), clients are far more likely to engage and stay in therapy when they feel their cultural identity is acknowledged and respected. Attempts at neutrality in these cases can come across as invalidation, or erasure.

We cannot pretend we are unaffected observers. We are participants, and our presence either heals or distances.

This does not mean we should blur boundaries or act on every emotional impulse. But it does mean we are to be honest with ourselves and with those we serve about the fact that our subjectivity is part of the room.

It's not about neutrality. It's about integrity.

Chart: Neutrality vs. Attuned Presence

This chart contrasts the difference between traditional ideas of 'clinical neutrality' and the more effective stance of attuned presence. It clarifies how neutrality, while well-intended, can unintentionally lead to emotional distance or invalidation.

Dimension	Neutrality	Attuned Presence
Tone	Flat or professional detachment	Warm, responsive, regulated
Emotional Safety	Minimizes expression to avoid bias	Acknowledges and holds emotional reality
Cultural Relevance	Avoids identity-related topics	Invites meaningful conversation about culture and identity
Response to Pain	Non-reactive and observational	Empathic, reflective, and supportive
Power Dynamics	Maintains distance as 'equalizer'	Shares power through authentic relationship

Integrity means we do our own work. We reflect on what we bring into the room. We examine our countertransference. We name the dynamics we might be enacting, even unknowingly.

True professionalism is not found in detachment; rather, it's found in intentional presence. It's in the capacity to be fully human, while also aware, grounded, and responsible.

When we let go of the myth of neutrality, we make space for something far more powerful: authentic connection.

And it is this connection, not perfection, that becomes the most healing element of all.

Diagram: The Myth of Objectivity Pyramid

This conceptual diagram shows how the idea of neutrality is shaped and reinforced by deeper systems of bias. It encourages reflection on the layers influencing our 'objective' stance.

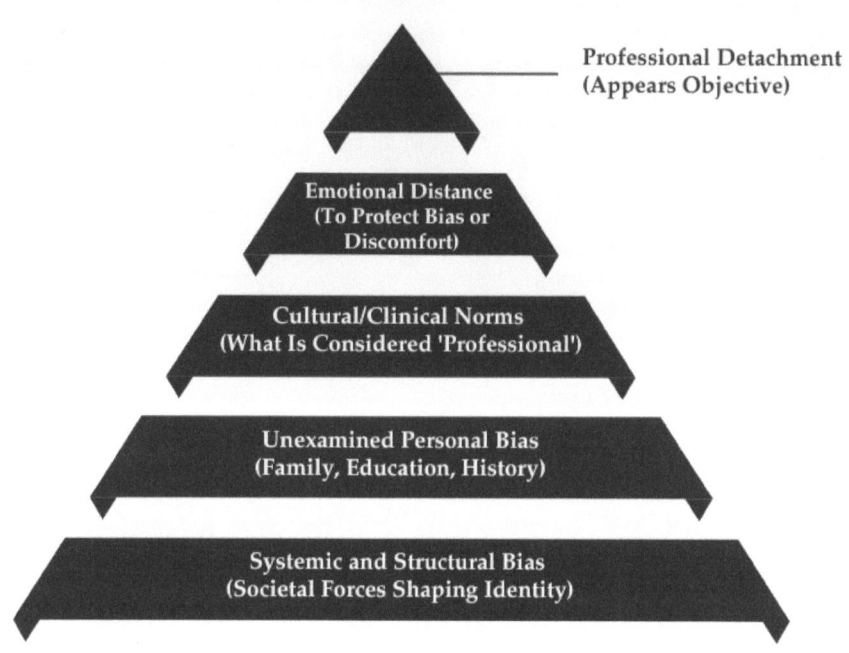

Reflection Prompts

- When have you leaned on the idea of 'neutrality' to avoid discomfort?
- How might the people you work with perceive your neutrality? As safety, or as absence?
- What would it look like to be fully present, engaged, and authentic — without overstepping boundaries?

References

- Horvath, A. O., Del Re, A. C., Flückiger, C., & Symonds, D. (2011). Alliance in individual psychotherapy. Psychotherapy, 48(1), 9–16.
- Sue, S., Capodilupo, C. M., Torino, G. C., Bucceri, J. M., Holder, A. M. B., Nadal, K. L., & Esquilin, M. (2007). Racial microaggressions in everyday life: Implications for clinical practice. American Psychologist, 62(4), 271–286.

Chapter 7 – Unconditional Positive Regard—And Why It's So Rare

"It is a rare gift to be deeply seen and accepted, not for who we could be, but for who we are, right now."

Carl Rogers, one of the pioneers of humanistic psychology, proposed that unconditional positive regard is one of the core conditions necessary for therapeutic change (Rogers, 1957).

Chart: Conditional vs. Unconditional Regard

This chart illustrates the difference between conditional and unconditional positive regard. It highlights how subtle shifts in language and mindset can influence the therapeutic relationship and client outcomes.

Dimension	Conditional Regard	Attuned Presence
Value Assignment	Earned through performance, progress, or compliance	Warm, responsive, regulated
Language	"I'm proud of you because you followed the plan."	Acknowledges and holds emotional reality
Response to Setbacks	Disappointment or withdrawal	Invites meaningful conversation about culture and identity
Underlying Belief	You're worthy if you meet expectations	Empathic, reflective, and supportive
Emotional Tone	Transactional, evaluative	Shares power through authentic relationship

To offer it means to accept someone completely, without judgment, without conditions, and without needing them to be different in order to be worthy of care.

But this kind of acceptance is exceedingly rare—not because we lack compassion, but because we are human.

We all carry expectations. We all have judgments, often hidden beneath layers of professionalism. We are taught to evaluate, diagnose, and intervene; but rarely are we taught to accept.

Yet research across disciplines confirms that acceptance, when genuine, is one of the most healing forces in human development.

Attachment theory shows that children who experience consistent acceptance develop more secure relationships, better emotional regulation, and greater resilience (Cassidy & Shaver, 2008). The same applies to adults.

In clinical settings, studies have shown that perceived empathy and acceptance predict stronger therapeutic alliances and better treatment outcomes (Elliott et al., 2011).

So why is it so hard to practice?

Because offering unconditional positive regard requires that we first offer it to ourselves.

It means seeing our own flaws and not turning away. It means recognizing our own wounds and still extending care. It means acknowledging our history, our conditioning, and our limitations without shame.

Most of us have never received this kind of regard. We've been loved with conditions, validated for performance, and accepted for compliance.

So, when we are asked to offer something we've never fully known, we freeze. We judge. We withhold.

This is why clinician self-awareness and personal healing are not luxuries—they are ethical imperatives.

We can only meet others to the extent we've met ourselves. We can only hold others if we've learned how to hold our own complexity with compassion.

Barriers to Unconditional Positive Regard (UPR) and How to Overcome Them

This infographic outlines common barriers that prevent practitioners from offering UPR, along with strategies to address them. Use it for personal reflection or team discussion.

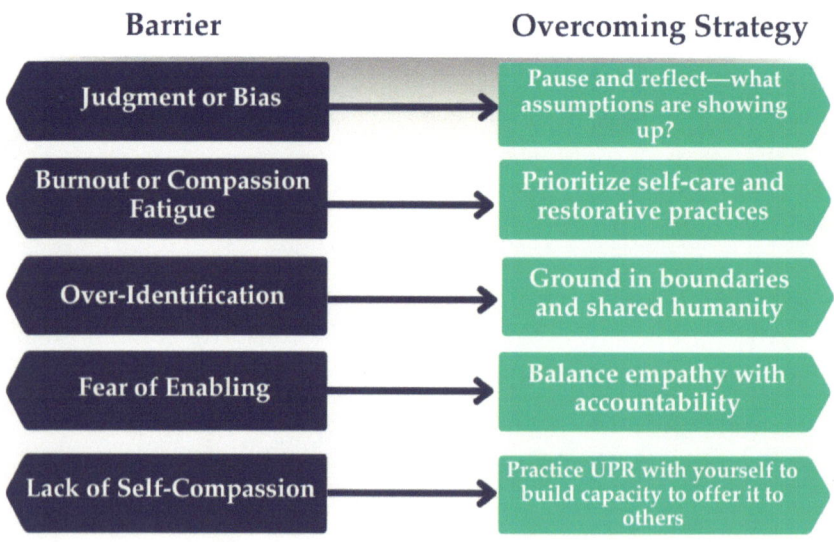

Barrier	Overcoming Strategy
Judgment or Bias	Pause and reflect—what assumptions are showing up?
Burnout or Compassion Fatigue	Prioritize self-care and restorative practices
Over-Identification	Ground in boundaries and shared humanity
Fear of Enabling	Balance empathy with accountability
Lack of Self-Compassion	Practice UPR with yourself to build capacity to offer it to others

Unconditional positive regard does not mean enabling. It does not mean agreeing. It does not mean denying harm or overlooking accountability.

It means this: you are still worthy of dignity, no matter where you are on your journey.

When people feel this—genuinely feel this, they begin to heal.

Because for many, it is the first time they are not being asked to earn love, to justify worth, or to prove value.

It is the first time someone has said—not with words but with presence— *"You don't have to be anything other than what you are for me to care."*

And that moment changes everything.

Reflection Prompts
- When was the last time you offered yourself unconditional positive regard?
- Who in your practice feels hard to accept right now? What might that be reflecting back to you?
- What would shift in your work if your presence alone communicated, 'You are already enough'?

References

- Cassidy, J., & Shaver, P. R. (2008). Handbook of Attachment: Theory, Research, and Clinical Applications (2nd ed.). The Guilford Press.
- Elliott, R., Bohart, A. C., Watson, J. C., & Greenberg, L. S. (2011). Empathy. Psychotherapy, 48(1), 43–49.
- Rogers, C. R. (1957). The necessary and sufficient conditions of therapeutic personality change. Journal of Consulting Psychology, 21(2), 95–103.

Chapter 8 – We Can't Give What We Don't Have

"You cannot pour from an empty cup. And you cannot offer what you've never received or practiced yourself."

It is a universal truth in healing work: we give from the inside out.

No matter our training, our credentials, or our best intentions, what we offer to others is deeply influenced by what we have cultivated within ourselves.

We cannot offer genuine calm if we have not learned to soothe our own nervous system. We cannot extend deep compassion if we are cruel to our own inner world.

And we cannot truly believe in someone else's healing if we've given up on our own.

This isn't a flaw; rather, it's a mirror. One that invites us to pause, reflect, and turn inward.

Self-compassion, self-regard, self-awareness—these are not just personal growth goals. They are clinical tools.

When clinicians are able to extend kindness to themselves, they are more present, less reactive, and more effective in the room (Neff & Germer, 2013).

Tool: Inner Inventory for Healers

This reflection tool helps practitioners identify their current internal state and how it might impact their work. Use this to enhance self-awareness, improve emotional regulation, and foster therapeutic presence.

INVENTORY AREA	CURRENT REFLECTION
Self-regard (How do I speak to myself under stress?)	
Boundaries (Do I feel overextended or clear?)	
Emotional availability (Am I present or shut down?)	
Energy level (Where is my tank—full, neutral, or empty?)	
Connection to purpose (Do I remember why I do this work?)	
Support systems (Am I getting support, or just giving it?)	

But without inner work, the very qualities that make us helpers—empathy, sensitivity, dedication, can become liabilities. They turn into burnout, boundary erosion, and unconscious reenactment.

Studies on clinician burnout show that lack of self-care, unresolved trauma, and emotional disconnection are core contributors to decreased empathy and poorer client outcomes (Shanafelt et al., 2015).

Our internal depletion doesn't just affect us. It ripples into our work.

When we are overextended, we stop seeing clearly. We go into autopilot. We rush sessions. We fall back on assumptions. We fail to attune.

All of this can undermine the very work we are trying to do.

There is nothing noble about martyrdom in healing professions. When we neglect our own healing, we diminish our capacity to offer it to others.

This doesn't mean we ought to be fully healed to help. It means we are to be in active relationship with our own humanity.

It means we stay aware of our triggers. We notice when we're projecting. We get support. We do the work we ask others to do.

In many ways, the most powerful gift we can offer is not expertise, but embodiment.

Chart: From Depletion to Embodiment

This chart outlines the contrast between burnout-driven interactions and embodied, self-connected care. Use it as a quick self-check or conversation starter in supervision or team meetings.

From Depletion to Embodiment

Dimension	Depletion State	Embodied State
Emotional Presence	Checked out, distracted	Present, attuned
Tone of Voice	Flat, tense, or reactive	Warm, grounded, calm
Capacity to Listen	Minimal, performative	Curious, spacious
Response to Challenge	Defensive, avoidant	Open, reflective
Sense of Meaning	Disconnected, mechanical	Aligned with purpose

When we model presence, when we practice regulation, when we speak to ourselves with kindness, we become a living invitation for others to do the same.

Healing begins within. And from there, it extends outward, in every interaction, every moment, and every silent message we send.

Because we teach, not just with our words, but with our way of being.

Reflection Prompts

- Where in your life are you asking others to do something you haven't fully practiced yourself?
- What are you offering your clients that you also need to offer to yourself?
- What might change in your work if you prioritized your inner healing as much as your clinical skill?

References

- Neff, K. D., & Germer, C. K. (2013). A pilot study and randomized controlled trial of the mindful self-compassion program. Journal of Clinical Psychology, 69(1), 28–44.
- Shanafelt, T. D., Boone, S., Tan, L., Dyrbye, L. N., Sotile, W., Satele, D., ... & Oreskovich, M. R. (2015). Burnout and satisfaction with work-life balance among US physicians relative to the general US population. Archives of Internal Medicine, 172(18), 1377–1385.

Chapter 9 – How Self-Regard Shapes Regard for Others

"The way we speak to ourselves sets the tone for how we speak to the world."

We tend to think of compassion as an outward act—something we give to others. But compassion begins with the way we relate to ourselves.

Self-regard—how we see, treat, and speak to ourselves, is the internal soil from which all other relationships grow.

If that soil is hostile, dry, or neglected, we will struggle to offer nourishment to others. Even if we try. Even if we care.

Our tone, our presence, our tolerance for discomfort—all are reflections of our inner landscape.

Research on self-compassion shows that individuals who practice kindness toward themselves are more likely to offer empathy, patience, and attunement in their relationships (Neff, 2003; Neff & Pommier, 2013).

Diagram: The Mirror Effect

This conceptual tool outlines how our inner relationship with ourselves mirrors outward into our interactions. Self-regard is the foundation of other-regard.

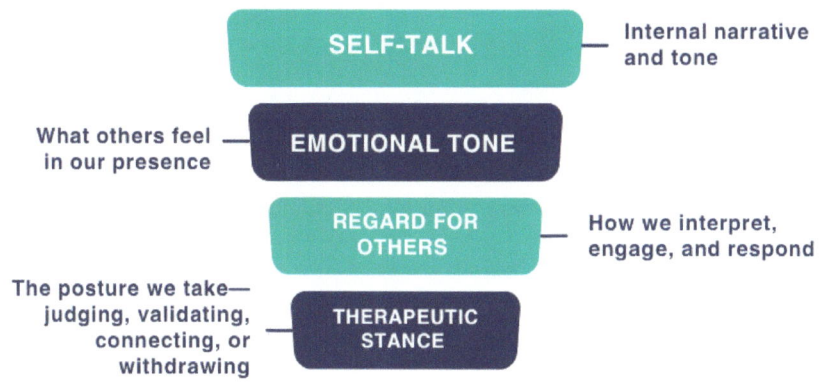

In contrast, those who are harsh, critical, or perfectionistic toward themselves are more likely to experience burnout, relational conflict, and reduced capacity for connection.

In clinical settings, this means that our internal dialogue becomes part of the therapeutic field.

When we're internally self-critical, we often hold others to unconscious standards. We expect quick change. We judge dependency. We misunderstand resistance.

We become impatient not just because of the other—but because we are impatient with ourselves.

Chart: Signs Your Inner Critic Is Driving the Work

When our inner critic is in the driver's seat, it can subtly shape how we show up with others. This chart helps identify warning signs and encourages a shift toward greater compassion and presence.

BEHAVIOR	DRIVEN BY INNER CRITIC	DRIVEN BY SELF-REGARD
Response to Client Resistance	Impatience or labeling	Curiosity and empathy
Mistakes in Practice	Self-blame, hiding, or defensiveness	Accountability and learning
Client Setbacks	Judgment or frustration	Compassion and recalibration
Supervision Dynamics	Over-explaining, performing	Openness and reflection
Emotional Presence	Guarded or performative	Authentic and grounded

Conversely, when we've cultivated compassion internally, we meet the moment differently. We're less reactive, more receptive; and we can hold ambiguity without needing to control it.

This doesn't mean we lose boundaries or stop striving. It means we lead from wholeness, not from woundedness.

A study by Gilbert & Procter (2006) on Compassion-Focused Therapy found that increasing self-compassion in clinicians not only improved their well-being but also enhanced their ability to build stronger therapeutic relationships.

This is the secret paradox of healing work: the more we turn inward with honesty and gentleness, the more present and powerful we become outwardly.

Our regard for others rises in proportion to the regard we offer ourselves.

And perhaps most importantly: the more we value our own humanity, the more precious we see in everyone else's.

Because ultimately, we do not heal people with techniques. We heal through who we are.

Reflection Prompts
- How do you speak to yourself after a difficult day of work?
- Where are you holding yourself to impossible standards that may also be showing up in your expectations of others?
- What would it look like to offer yourself the same regard you offer the people you serve?

References
- Neff, K. D. (2003). The development and validation of a scale to measure self-compassion. Self and Identity, 2(3), 223–250.
- Neff, K. D., & Pommier, E. (2013). The relationship between self-compassion and other-focused concern among college undergraduates, community adults, and practicing meditators. Self and Identity, 12(2), 160–176.
- Gilbert, P., & Procter, S. (2006). Compassionate mind training for people with high shame and self-criticism: Overview and pilot study of a group therapy approach. Clinical Psychology & Psychotherapy, 13(6), 353–379.

Chapter 10 – Soul-Searching in the Clinical Space

"We go into the depths of another's pain only to the degree we've dared to visit our own."

Clinical work is often thought of as objective, structured, evidence-based, and it should be.

But it is also deeply personal, emotional, and spiritual. It asks us not only to understand the human mind but to walk alongside human suffering.

This is why the work of helping, if done with honesty, always becomes a mirror.

Every client interaction, every challenging behavior, every emotional moment has the potential to show us something about ourselves.

And yet, many of us were trained to keep our inner world separate. To 'leave ourselves at the door.'

But healing doesn't work that way.

We don't just bring our tools—we bring our histories, our beliefs, our biases, our wounds. The more unconscious they are, the more power they hold over the work.

Soul-searching is the antidote.

It is the ongoing practice of turning inward—not for self-indulgence, but for clarity, integrity, and growth.

It is the willingness to ask: What is this moment stirring in me? Why is this person activating something? What part of my story might be showing up here?

Checklist: 12 Questions for Clinical Soul-Searching

Use this checklist regularly—in supervision, personal journaling, or team reflection—to stay grounded in presence, clarity, and growth. These questions are designed to deepen awareness and integrity in your practice.

- [ ] What emotion came up for me most often in my work this week?
- [ ] What moment did I feel most connected to someone I serve?
- [ ] When did I notice myself disengage or emotionally shut down?
- [ ] What assumptions have I made about someone's behavior or motivation?
- [ ] What belief did I bring into a room that may have shaped the outcome?
- [ ] What was I afraid to say—or feel?
- [ ] Where did I rush, and why?
- [ ] What did I fail to acknowledge in myself or someone else?
- [ ] How did my own story, history, or identity show up today?
- [ ] What feedback am I resisting, and what might it be pointing to?
- [ ] When did I choose presence over performance?
- [ ] What would it look like to bring more soul into my work tomorrow?

These questions are not distractions. They are the foundation of ethical, effective, human-centered care.

In psychoanalytic theory, the concept of 'use of self' refers to the clinician's capacity to consciously bring their own humanity into the room as a therapeutic tool (Baldwin, 2000). But we cannot use what we have not examined.

Research in relational therapies shows that clinician self-awareness and emotional insight significantly enhance the therapeutic alliance and reduce rupture (Safran & Muran, 2000).

But beyond data, this is about integrity. About aligning our inner and outer worlds so we don't split ourselves in the name of professionalism.

Soul-searching does not mean oversharing. It means staying awake. It means noticing when we're closed off. It means returning to presence, again and again.

Because the deeper we know ourselves, the more fully we can see — and serve — others.

And in the end, every act of healing is an invitation to both people in the room: to return to wholeness, to remember their worth, to walk each other home.

Framework: The Inside-Out Supervision Model

Supervision is most powerful when it supports both skill-building and self-awareness. This framework outlines an integrated approach to supervision that fosters presence, honesty, and professional growth.

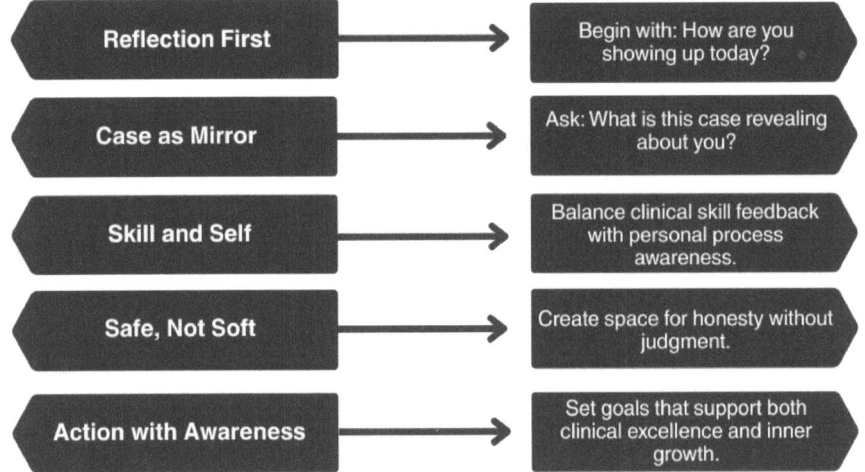

Reflection Prompts

- What emotional patterns tend to emerge for you in your work with others?
- What do you tend to avoid, emotionally, relationally, spiritually, in the clinical space?
- How might regular soul-searching strengthen your clarity, empathy, and presence?

References

- Baldwin, M. (2000). The use of self in therapy (2nd ed.). Routledge.
- Safran, J. D., & Muran, J. C. (2000). Negotiating the therapeutic alliance: A relational treatment guide. Guilford Press.

Chapter 11 – Inner Work as Professional Practice

"The most important work we do is the work we do on ourselves."

In nearly every profession, there is continuing education. We learn new tools, attend conferences, refine our techniques. But in the healing professions, continuing education ought to go deeper. Because the tool is not just the intervention—it is us.

Inner work is not extra. It is essential. And yet, most models of professional development focus only on external competence: knowledge, procedures, compliance. What often gets left out is the interior: the clinician's self-awareness, integrity, and emotional maturity.

Table: External vs. Internal Competence

This table compares outer skill-building with the equally vital but often overlooked inner competencies. Both are essential for ethical, effective, and sustainable practice.

DOMAIN	EXTERNAL COMPETENCE	INTERNAL COMPETENCE
Knowledge	Understanding evidence-based practices	Understanding personal values and triggers
Skill	Effective use of clinical techniques	Regulation of emotional and energetic presence
Assessment	Ability to analyze behavior and symptoms	Ability to reflect on one's own perception and bias
Communication	Clear and concise language	Curiosity, attunement, and deep listening
Decision-Making	Following protocols and best practices	Integrating gut sense and ethical reflection

This omission is costly. It leads to burnout, blind spots, boundary issues, and stagnation. According to Norcross and Lambert (2018), one of the most robust predictors of positive outcomes in therapy is the therapist's own level of personal development and psychological flexibility. This means that our effectiveness is shaped as much by who we are as by what we do. And who we are is not static. It is to be cultivated.

Inner work includes reflection, meditation, therapy, supervision, journaling, spiritual practice—any activity that deepens our awareness, increases our compassion, and grounds us in presence. When clinicians engage in these practices, they report higher levels of resilience, satisfaction, and connection to purpose (Shapiro et al., 2007).

Infographic: Inner Work = Ethical Work Cycle

This infographic outlines the ongoing relationship between inner growth and ethical impact. It is designed to encourage a professional development model rooted in presence and reflection.

Inner work is also the foundation of ethical practice. Without it, we risk acting from our wounds rather than our wisdom. We may misinterpret a client's behavior based on our unresolved issues. We may overidentify, under-respond, or rescue. And in systems where speed and productivity are prized, it takes courage to say: 'My inner clarity matters just as much as my outer output.' But it does. Because we set the emotional tone of the space. We co-create the field. Our nervous system affects theirs.

When we are present, grounded, and centered, we become a healing presence—not just a provider of services. This is the heart of trauma-informed care: not just changing what we do, but who we become. So let us treat inner work not as optional, but as professional responsibility, as clinical hygiene, and as leadership. Because when we do our work, we invite others to do theirs. And the field begins to shift—one encounter at a time.

Reflection Prompts

- What inner practices currently support your work? Which are missing?
- When have you noticed your inner state impacting your effectiveness?
- What would change if you prioritized inner work as part of your clinical routine?

References

- Norcross, J. C., & Lambert, M. J. (2018). Psychotherapy relationships that work (3rd ed.). Oxford University Press.
- Shapiro, S. L., Brown, K. W., & Biegel, G. M. (2007). Teaching self-care to caregivers: Effects of mindfulness-based stress reduction on the mental health of therapists in training. Training and Education in Professional Psychology, 1(2), 105–115.

Chapter 12 – From Fixing to Being With

"People are not problems to be solved – they are mysteries to be witnessed."

In the rush of clinical work, we are often trained to find solutions: to fix, to treat, to resolve. This action-oriented mindset is useful—it helps us stay focused, efficient, and goal-directed. But it also carries a shadow: it can pull us away from presence. From being with what is.

When we focus on fixing, we tend to see people as puzzles. Their symptoms as glitches. Their pain as something to eradicate. And in doing so, we may inadvertently send the message: 'You are not okay as you are.' But healing doesn't always come from doing. Often, it comes from being—with. Being with someone in their suffering, without needing to change it right away, is one of the most radical acts of care.

Diagram: Fixing Mode vs. Being-With Mode

This comparison outlines the difference between a problem-solving mindset and a relational, presence-based approach. Use this visual to reorient your stance in moments of urgency or emotional intensity.

DIMENSION	FIXING MODE	BEING-WITH MODE
Goal	Solve the Problem	Hold the Experience
Focus	Behavior or Symptom	Emotional Meaning and Context
Pace	Urgent, Rushed	Slow, Spacious
Tone	Directive, Corrective	Validating, Attuned
Underlying Message	You must change to be ok	You are enough to be with as you are

Research on the therapeutic alliance shows that empathy, attunement, and presence are more predictive of outcomes than specific techniques (Wampold, 2015). In palliative care, where 'fixing' is no longer an option, presence becomes the medicine. The same principle applies in mental health. When we slow down, breathe, and listen deeply, we offer safety. We offer acknowledgment. We offer dignity.

This is not passive—it is active presence. It requires more strength than rushing in with solutions. Because to be with someone in their pain, without flinching, requires that we've made peace with our own. This is why 'fixing' can sometimes be a defense, a way to avoid our own discomfort with powerlessness.

But our task is not to rescue—it is to accompany, to bear witness, and to walk with. When we shift from fixing to being with, we stop trying to steer someone's journey and start honoring it. We become facilitators of discovery, not directors of outcomes. And in doing so, we create the conditions for real, lasting transformation, because we are not pushing change from the outside; we are cultivating safety from the inside.

Tool: 3-Step Presence Practice for Attuned Engagement

This tool helps you pause, ground, and shift into relational presence before or during a challenging interaction.

In the words of Carl Rogers, 'The curious paradox is that when I accept myself just as I am, then I can change.' What if the same is true for those we serve?

Reflection Prompts

- In your work, when do you tend to move into 'fix-it' mode?
- What would it look like to simply be with someone, without trying to solve their pain?
- What part of yourself might you need to accept more fully in order to offer that same acceptance to others?

References

- Wampold, B. E. (2015). How important are the common factors in psychotherapy? An update. World Psychiatry, 14(3), 270–277.
- Rogers, C. R. (1961). On becoming a person: A therapist's view of psychotherapy. Houghton Mifflin Harcourt.

Chapter 13 – Presence as Intervention

"Sometimes the most therapeutic thing we can do is to truly show up."

In a world obsessed with doing, we often underestimate the power of simply being. Yet presence, the quality of our attention, our openness, our groundedness, is one of the most potent healing forces we can offer. Presence is not passive. It is active attunement. It says: 'I see you. I'm here. I'm not going anywhere.'

Neurologically, this kind of presence activates the parasympathetic nervous system, helping people shift from a state of threat to a state of safety (Porges, 2011). In trauma-informed care, presence serves as a stabilizing anchor. It communicates safety through tone, posture, rhythm, and regulation—not just through words.

Framework: The Presence Triangle

The Presence Triangle illustrates the three core elements that support therapeutic presence. Use this as a guide for cultivating a grounding and healing atmosphere in your daily work.

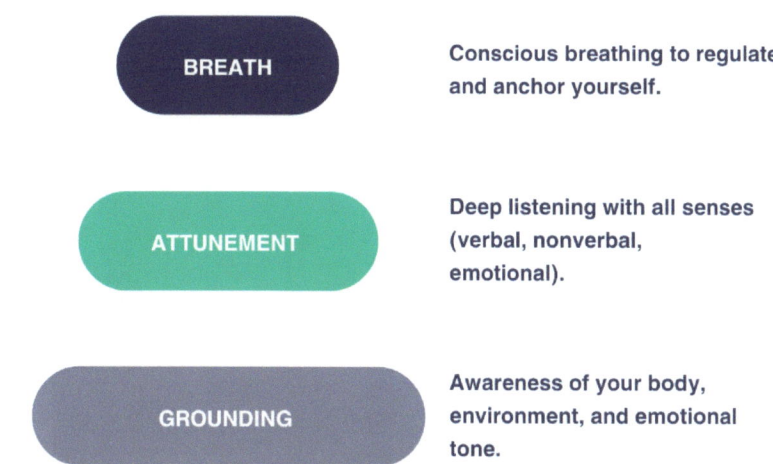

Research on right-brain-to-right-brain communication shows that nonverbal presence—eye contact, facial expression, timing, plays a critical role in affect regulation and attachment repair (Schore, 2009). This is especially important when working with individuals whose histories include abandonment, neglect, or relational trauma. For them, presence is not a neutral event—it is a corrective emotional experience. It rebuilds trust in small, often invisible ways.

And for clinicians, cultivating presence means we are to be in touch with our own body, breath, and awareness. It requires slowing down, letting go of the rush to fix, tolerating silence. In mindfulness-based therapies, presence is both the foundation and the goal. It is what allows clinicians to respond, rather than react, to listen, rather than anticipate, to be, rather than perform.

Infographic: What Presence Looks Like vs. What It Feels Like

This table provides examples of observable behaviors and the emotional impact they often produce. Use this to strengthen awareness of how your energy and attention are being received.

BEHAVIOR	LOOKS LIKE	FEELS LIKE (TO THE OTHER PERSON
Eye Contact	Soft, steady, and non-intrusive	Seen, acknowledged
Body Orientation	Facing toward the person, open posture	Welcomed, respected
Pacing	Unrushed, with pauses and silence	Safe, not pressured
Tone of Voice	Calm, clear, emotionally congruent	Soothed, validated
Breath & Presence	Breathing evenly, grounded stance	Stability, calm energy

When clinicians cultivate presence, they report reduced burnout, increased clinical effectiveness, and stronger therapeutic alliances (Geller & Greenberg, 2012). Presence is not something we give; it's something we become. And when we become it, people feel it. They soften. They settle. They begin to open. Because before they trust our interventions, they trust our being. And that trust, that safety, that precious space between two nervous systems, is where healing begins.

Reflection Prompts
- What does presence mean to you — not just conceptually, but somatically?
- When do you feel most grounded and present in your work?
- What small shifts could you make to deepen your presence in each interaction?

References
- Porges, S. W. (2011). The polyvagal theory: Neurophysiological foundations of emotions, attachment, communication, and self-regulation. W. W. Norton & Company.
- Schore, A. N. (2009). Right-brain affect regulation: An essential mechanism of development, trauma, dissociation, and psychotherapy. In D. Fosha, D. J. Siegel, & M. F. Solomon (Eds.), The healing power of emotion (pp. 112–144). W. W. Norton & Company.
- Geller, S. M., & Greenberg, L. S. (2012). Therapeutic presence: A mindful approach to effective therapy. American Psychological Association.

Chapter 14 – Belief as Medicine

"The moment we believe in someone's potential, we become part of their healing."

Belief is more than a feeling. It is a force. It shapes what we see, how we speak, what we expect, and what we invite others to become. In the healing professions, our belief in someone's capacity to grow may be one of the most powerful, underutilized interventions we possess. It influences tone, pacing, treatment goals, engagement, and ultimately, outcome. The Pygmalion effect, the phenomenon in which higher expectations lead to improved performance, has been documented in education, medicine, and psychotherapy (Rosenthal & Jacobson, 1968; Snyder, 1984). People rise or fall, in part, based on the subtle signals they receive about what is possible.

Chart: Belief-Based Practice vs. Behavior-Based Practice

This chart contrasts two orientations to care: one that centers internal belief and one that focuses solely on external behavior. Use it to reframe moments when a shift in belief may lead to better outcomes.

DOMAIN	BEHAVIOR-BASED PRACTICE	BELIEF-BASED PRACTICE
Focus	What they are doing	Who they are becoming
Assessment	Compliance, output, attendance	Context, growth, effort
Intervention	Correct, redirect, reward	Explore, believe, collaborate
Tone	Evaluative and reactive	Curious and relational
Outcome	Behavior change under pressure	Sustainable transformation through trust

When a clinician truly believes in someone's ability to recover, transform, and thrive, that belief radiates. It shows up in the eyes, the posture, the presence. It shows up in the way we sit with them in their pain without rushing, in the way we hold hope when they cannot. Hope, like despair, is contagious. And belief is the conduit. In motivational interviewing, one of the foundational principles is to support self-efficacy, the belief that change is possible (Miller & Rollnick, 2013). But we cannot support what we do not hold ourselves.

Flowchart: Belief Transmission in the Helping Relationship

This flowchart illustrates how our internal belief system influences what others experience—and how belief can serve as a healing intervention in and of itself.

BELIEF TRANSMISSION IN THE HELPING RELATIONSHIP

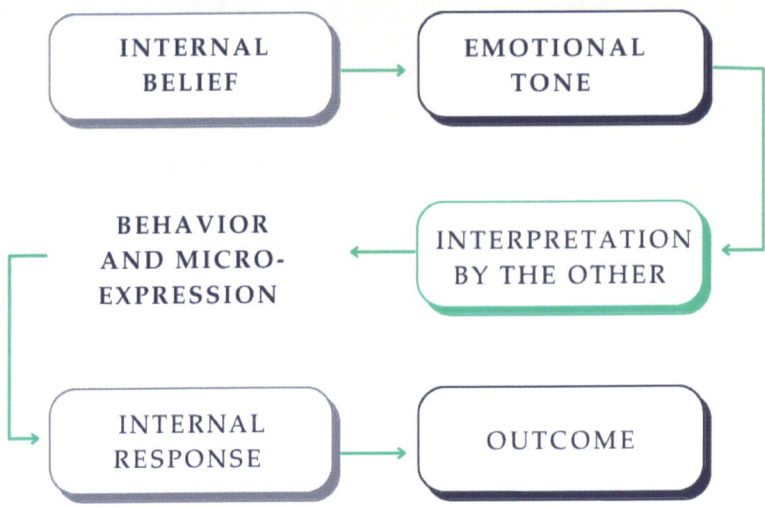

If we've stopped believing in someone's potential, we will withdraw—energetically, emotionally, or relationally. And people feel it. This doesn't mean we lie or offer false hope. It means we hold a deeper knowing: that no one is ever beyond the reach of growth. That change is not linear. That setbacks do not define identity.

Belief as medicine is not about denying reality; rather, it's about expanding it. It's about seeing not just the diagnosis, but the person. It's about seeing not just the behavior, but the wound, not just the present, but the possible. We do this not with grand gestures, but with subtle consistency: seeing, hearing, validating, and staying. Because sometimes, belief is the only medicine someone has never received. And once they taste it, even a drop, they begin to believe in themselves.

Reflection Prompts

- Think of someone in your care. What do you truly believe is possible for them?
- Are there individuals for whom your belief has quietly diminished? What might help reignite it?
- What do you believe about your own capacity to grow, evolve, and heal?

References

- Miller, W. R., & Rollnick, S. (2013). Motivational interviewing: Helping people change (3rd ed.). Guilford Press.
- Rosenthal, R., & Jacobson, L. (1968). Pygmalion in the classroom: Teacher expectation and pupils' intellectual development. Holt, Rinehart & Winston.
- Snyder, C. R. (1984). The psychology of hope: You can get there from here. Free Press.

Chapter 15 – Building a New Therapeutic Paradigm

"We are not just clinicians. We are culture-shapers. And the culture of care begins with us."

The time has come for a shift in the way we approach healing — not just in theory, but in practice, relationship, and presence. We are living in a moment of reckoning. Systems are strained. Burnout is high. Disconnection is everywhere. And yet, the potential for something new is emerging. The future of care is not found in more complex protocols or endless documentation. It is found in returning to what is most human: belief, presence, relationship, and integrity. The next therapeutic paradigm is to be one that centers the whole person — both the one being served and the one serving. It is to honor the reality that healing is not a transaction — it is a co-created process rooted in safety, connection, and authenticity.

This new paradigm asks us to let go of outdated notions of neutrality, fixing, and emotional distance. Instead, it invites us into a deeper alignment with our values: to see people not as problems, but as stories; not as diagnoses, but as souls; not as cases, but as fellow humans navigating pain and possibility. It also invites us to be brave, to do our own work, to name our blind spots, and to reflect on how our presence is shaping the outcomes we see. This is not soft. This is rigorous. It asks for courage, honesty, and a redefinition of professionalism — not as stoicism, but as integrated wholeness.

From System-Centered to Human-Centered Care

This visual illustrates the shift from traditional, compliance-driven systems of care to approaches centered on humanity, connection, and belief.

DOMAIN	SYSTEM-CENTERED MODEL	HUMAN-CENTERED PARADIGM
Primary Goal	Stability, compliance, control	Healing, connection, trust
Client Identity	Case, diagnosis, number	Whole person, story, potential
Success Measured By	Attendance, documentation	Growth, insight, relationship quality
Clinician Role	Expert, fixer, authority	Guide, witness, partner
Underlying Belief	We know what's best	People carry their own wisdom
Relational Style	Transactional, scripted	Relational, co-created

As we build this paradigm, we draw on the best of science and the wisdom of humanity. From interpersonal neurobiology to attachment theory, from motivational interviewing to mindfulness, the evidence is clear: relationships heal. Safety heals. Attunement heals. And all of that begins with us. We are the medicine. Our presence is the intervention. Our belief is the catalyst. Let us build systems that reflect this truth, not just in language, but in structure. Not just in training, but in culture.

Let us cultivate environments where those who serve are supported in doing their own inner work—where supervision includes reflection, where leadership models presence, where policies are shaped by compassion.

This is how we break the cycles of disconnection. This is how we build trust. This is how we shift outcomes—one interaction, one moment, one belief at a time. Because the work of healing is not just about what we do—it's about who we become while doing it.

Visual Summary: The 10 Commitments of the New Therapeutic Paradigm

Use these 10 commitments as guiding principles for culture change, supervision, training, and practice.

- [ ] Lead with belief, not judgment.
- [ ] See the human before the behavior.
- [ ] Practice presence as your first intervention.
- [ ] Assume logic in every action.
- [ ] Center relationships over compliance.
- [ ] Use power to elevate, not control.
- [ ] Stay curious, especially when challenged.
- [ ] Validate before redirecting.
- [ ] Reflect before reacting.
- [ ] Make space for your own humanity—then offer that same space to others.

Reflection Prompts

- What kind of healing culture are you creating through your presence, language, and actions?
- What parts of the old paradigm are you still holding onto? What might it be time to release?
- What does a more human, more honest, and more healing way of working look like for you?

References

- Siegel, D. J. (2012). The developing mind: How relationships and the brain interact to shape who we are. Guilford Press.
- Geller, S. M., & Greenberg, L. S. (2012). Therapeutic presence: A mindful approach to effective therapy. American Psychological Association.
- Miller, W. R., & Rollnick, S. (2013). Motivational interviewing: Helping people change (3rd ed.). Guilford Press.

Epilogue

This work is never really done.

The work of healing, of helping, of holding space — for others, and for ourselves — doesn't have an endpoint. It unfolds moment by moment, encounter by encounter, breath by breath.

What this book has tried to show is simple, but not easy: that we are not separate from the outcomes we seek. We are part of the story, part of the pattern, and, most importantly, part of the possibility.

The more we do our own inner work, the more others feel seen.

The more we see our own blind spots, the more we create safety.

The more we offer ourselves compassion, the more we extend it outward.

This is how systems change.

Not only through policy or funding — but through presence, through relationship, through the quiet revolution of people who choose to see with new eyes.

May we keep choosing to see, to believe, and to stay open.

Because the truth is, the healing we're waiting for may already be here.

It may have already begun.

Because of Us.

Conclusion – We Are the Variable

"The healing we offer others can only be as deep as the healing we allow within ourselves."

By now, you've journeyed through the invisible landscape of clinical work: the unseen beliefs, the unconscious biases, the subtle ways our presence becomes either a bridge or a barrier to healing. This book was not written to give you more techniques. It was written to remind you of what you already carry — and to help you see it more clearly.

Because you matter. Your energy. Your story. Your belief. Your self-regard. Your capacity to stay, to feel, to reflect. These are not side notes. They are the medicine. And every time you enter the room, you bring all of that with you — consciously or not.

The future of healing doesn't lie in more productivity, more efficiency, or more paperwork. It lies in returning to our humanity. In seeing ourselves and others with more depth, more honesty, and more compassion.

This is not soft work. It is precious work. It asks us to feel things we'd rather avoid, to admit when we've become mechanical, to question what we've been taught, and to reflect on who we are becoming. It also offers hope. Because if healing is about relationship, and we are part of that relationship, then we are not powerless. We are part of the solution.

Every moment of presence. Every shift in belief. Every act of self-reflection has a ripple effect. Because when we do our inner work, the outer work begins to transform—quietly, steadily, and often profoundly. So let us carry forward what this book has invited:

To examine our part, to soften our stance, to own our influence, and to deepen our practice—not only for others, but for ourselves. Because in the end, healing happens not only because of what we do—but because of us.

A Note to the Reader

Thank you for taking the time to journey through this book. If it moved you, challenged you, or opened something new inside you, we invite you to keep going—because this isn't the end. It's an opening.

The SWEET Institute exists to help you deepen the very transformation this book speaks to. Through trainings, coaching, community, and publishing, we help people like you show up with presence, purpose, and power—in life and in work.

Take a moment now. What insight from this book will you carry into your next conversation? What shift in belief will you commit to practice? What part of you is ready to be reclaimed and shared?

Your growth is not just personal. It's collective. And the more you live from that place, the more others are liberated too.

We invite you to explore more of what SWEET offers: learning experiences that speak to the heart, challenge the intellect, and catalyze deep, sustainable change.

And if this book resonated with you, please help us spread the message:

> → Share it with a colleague or supervisor.

> → Bring it to your team meetings or learning circles.

> → Leave a thoughtful review on Amazon or wherever you purchased it.

Your voice helps amplify the healing. Your story helps others say yes to their own.

For more on SWEET Institute Publishing or to share your feedback, reflections, or book ideas, visit:

www.SWEETInstitutePublishing.com.

Together, we are redefining healing, one reader at a time.

> — **SWEET Institute**

Final Acknowledgments

As this book comes to a close, I offer a final word of thanks to those whose impact may never fully be named—but is deeply felt.

To the unseen supporters—the administrative assistants, janitors, security staff, outreach teams, and behind-the-scenes hands who keep our systems moving—thank you. You make the work possible, and you rarely get the credit you deserve.

To the mentors who challenged us, the peers who walked beside us, and the critics who helped us sharpen our clarity—thank you for your presence on this path.

To the readers—thank you for daring to go within. May this book become not just something you read, but something you practice, embody, and share.

And finally, to the spirit of service itself—that quiet call that lives in the hearts of those who choose to care—you are the reason we keep going. You are the pulse of this work.

May we never forget: The most powerful change begins because of us.

Reader Integration Toolkit

1. Daily Reflection Prompts

- What did I assume today without realizing it?
- Did I truly listen, or was I waiting to respond?
- Who did I believe in today — and who did I silently doubt?
- Where did I show up fully? Where did I hold back?

2. Weekly Practice

- Choose one patient, or client, or resident, and approach them with a mindset of full belief.
- Slow down during one interaction this week. Make eye contact. Pause before you speak.
- Keep a presence journal: Note moments you felt connected, disconnected, reactive, or grounded.

3. Team Discussion Questions

- How do our own stories shape the way we interpret others' behavior?
- What is one blind spot I might have when working with those we serve?
- How do we reinforce or disrupt disempowering narratives in our teams?

4. Monthly Integration Challenge

- Host a *'Because of Us'* reflection circle at your site or agency.
- Pair up with a colleague to offer each other feedback on presence, tone, and regard.
- Choose one chapter to re-read and apply its lesson daily for a week.

5. SWEET Institute Tools to Support You

- Attend a live training on Belief-Based Practice or Healing-Centered Engagement.
- Use the SWEET Validation Framework in your next team meeting (Appendix B)
- Download the SWEET Clinical Reflection Card Deck (Available upon request)

Appendix

(Tools, exercises, charts, and Frameworks)

Appendix A

1. The Belief-Result Pathway Framework
- Belief → Perception → Emotional Tone → Action → Result
- Use this to trace outcomes backward to their originating beliefs.

2. Daily Self-Check Tool
- What belief am I holding about this person right now?
- How is that belief shaping my tone, body language, or assumptions?
- Is this belief helping or harming the relationship?

3. The Presence Pause Exercise
- **Step 1**: Stop and take three slow breaths before each key interaction.
- **Step 2**: Silently say, 'This person is doing the best they can right now.'
- **Step 3**: Begin the conversation with full attention and curiosity.

4. Chart: Conditional vs. Unconditional Regard
- **Conditional**: Based on compliance, performance, or behavior.
- **Unconditional**: Based on intrinsic worth, humanity, and shared dignity.

5. Team Reflection Template
- One belief I held this week that was challenged:

- One thing I did differently because of that shift:
- One person I now see with greater compassion:

6. Cognitive Reorganization Technique
- Identify → Interrupt → Replace → Reinforce
- E.g., 'They're resistant' becomes 'They're protecting something important to them.'

7. Chart: Healing Behaviors vs. Harmful Habits
- **Healing Behaviors**: Listening, validating, empowering, reflecting, pausing.
- **Harmful Habits**: Rushing, labeling, correcting, assuming, reacting.

8. Monthly Team Integration Plan
- Week 1: Read one chapter as a team.
- Week 2: Practice the Presence Pause daily.
- Week 3: Use the Team Reflection Template.
- Week 4: Host a peer dialogue or integration circle.

Appendix B – SWEET Validation Framework

The SWEET Validation Framework is a foundational approach to trauma-informed, person-centered engagement. It supports therapeutic connection, staff effectiveness, and meaningful outcomes by prioritizing the core human need to feel seen, heard, and understood.

Core Principle

Before anything else, validate.

The 5 Core Components of the SWEET Validation Framework

1. See the Human First

Recognize the person's dignity, history, pain, and humanity before focusing on behavior, symptoms, or goals.

→ **Example**: "I see you."

2. Name the Emotional Experience

Reflect back the feeling behind the words or actions, without judgment or interpretation.

→ **Example**: "It sounds like this has been overwhelming."

3. Affirm the Logic or Function

Every behavior makes sense in context. Reflect back the internal logic—even if the behavior is harmful.

→ **Example**: "It makes sense that you'd want to protect yourself that way."

4. Normalize the Reaction

Remind the person that what they're feeling is human and understandable given the circumstances.

→ **Example**: "Anyone in your situation might feel the same way."

5. Invite Agency and Partnership

Shift from fixing to working with. Empower the person to take the next step with support.

→ **Example**: "Tell me what you think would help now."

Evidence Base

The SWEET Validation Framework integrates multiple evidence-based models, including:
- Carl Rogers' Unconditional Positive Regard (Rogers, 1957)
- Marsha Linehan's Validation Strategies in DBT (Linehan, 1993)
- Stephen Porges' Polyvagal Theory (Porges, 2011)
- Trauma-Informed Care Principles (SAMHSA, 2014)
- Motivational Interviewing (Miller & Rollnick, 2013)

Applications
- 1:1 conversation with patients or clients
- De-escalation and crisis response
- Supervision and reflective practice
- Team meetings and interdisciplinary collaboration
- Documentation and care planning
- Organizational culture and training

Recommended Reading

- Rogers, Carl R. (1961). On Becoming a Person: A Therapist's View of Psychotherapy.
- Linehan, Marsha. (2015). DBT Skills Training Manual (2nd ed.).
- Van der Kolk, Bessel. (2014). The Body Keeps the Score: Brain, Mind, and Body in the Healing of Trauma.
- Siegel, Daniel J. (2010). The Mindful Therapist: A Clinician's Guide to Mindsight and Neural Integration.
- Dweck, Carol S. (2006). Mindset: The New Psychology of Success.
- Miller, William R., & Rollnick, Stephen. (2013). Motivational Interviewing: Helping People Change (3rd ed.).
- Porges, Stephen W. (2017). The Pocket Guide to the Polyvagal Theory: The Transformative Power of Feeling Safe.
- Brown, Brené. (2018). Dare to Lead: Brave Work. Tough Conversations. Whole Hearts.
- Cozolino, Louis. (2017). The Neuroscience of Psychotherapy: Healing the Social Brain (3rd ed.).
- Kabat-Zinn, Jon. (1990). Full Catastrophe Living: Using the Wisdom of Your Body and Mind to Face Stress, Pain, and Illness.

More from SWEET Institute Publishing

SWEET Institute Publishing offers transformational books designed to foster awareness, empower, and guide professionals, practitioners, and leaders through the art and science of healing. Each title is rooted in evidence, experience, and empathy, bridging clinical insight with human wisdom.

Explore our other titles:

- Before Anything Else, Validate – A revolutionary guide to healing relationships through the power of validation. (Upcoming)
- The Kindness Imperative – How power becomes purpose, and why true greatness begins with grace. (Upcoming)
- Breaking the Pattern – Understanding and healing repetition compulsion using the topographical model.
- Freeing Fear – A journey through the conscious, preconscious, and unconscious to reclaim courage.
- The Courage to Care – Stories of healing, hope, and the power of social work.
- The Still Point – Where presence, peace, and purpose converge to transform every area of life.
- How Life Works – What every challenge, pattern, and lesson is trying to teach you—about growth, joy, and mastery.
- The Simplicity Principle – Learn faster, live lighter, and lead with clarity by breaking everything down.

Visit www.SWEETInstitutePublishing.com to browse our full catalog, join our newsletter, and submit your own manuscript ideas. Together, we are building a world of conscious, compassionate change — one book at a time.

About the Authors

Mardoche Sidor, M.D.

Dr. Mardoche Sidor is a Harvard-trained, quadruple board-certified psychiatrist and former Assistant Professor of Clinical Psychiatry at Columbia University, Vagelos College of Physicians and Surgeons, and maintains an academic affiliation with Columbia University Center for Psychoanalytic Training and Research. Born and raised in Haiti, his early experiences ignited a profound commitment to healing and service. Dr. Sidor has served in various capacities, including primary care physician and Chief Medical Officer at the Center for Alternative Sentencing and Employment Services (CASES). He is the founder and CEO of the SWEET Institute, an organization dedicated to transforming mental health education and practice. An accomplished author, Dr. Sidor has penned dozens of books and hundreds of articles, contributing significantly to the field of mental health.

Karen Dubin, Ph.D., LCSW

Dr. Karen Dubin is a Columbia-trained social worker with over two decades of experience in clinical practice, teaching, supervision, and leadership. She has held executive roles in both public and private sectors, including Chief Operating Officer at the SWEET Institute. Dr. Dubin is renowned for her expertise in adult mental health, trauma treatment, and advocacy for marginalized populations. She has contributed to over dozens of books and hundreds of articles and serves as adjunct faculty at Columbia University and Adelphi University.

Together, Drs. Sidor and Dubin co-founded the SWEET Institute, combining their extensive experience to create a transformative platform for mental health professionals and agencies. Their collaborative work emphasizes empowerment, resilience, and the profound impact of belief in the healing process.

www.ingramcontent.com/pod-product-compliance
Lightning Source LLC
Chambersburg PA
CBHW042331150426
43194CB00001B/15